LIT'
BIT'

ANDREW MARSHALL, JR.

Copyright © 2024 Andrew Marshall, Jr..

All rights reserved. No part of this book may be reproduced, stored, or transmitted by any means—whether auditory, graphic, mechanical, or electronic—without written permission of both publisher and author, except in the case of brief excerpts used in critical articles and reviews. Unauthorized reproduction of any part of this work is illegal and is punishable by law.

ISBN: 978-1-63950-259-2 (sc)
ISBN: 978-1-63950-267-7 (e)

This publication contains the opinions and ideas of its author. It is intended to provide helpful and informative material on the subjects addressed in the publication. The author and publisher specifically disclaim all responsibility for any liability, loss, or risk, personal or otherwise, which is incurred as a consequence, directly or indirectly, of the use and application of any of the contents of this book.

Writers Apex

Gateway Towards Success

8063 MADISON AVE #1252
Indianapolis, IN 46227
+13176596889
www.writersapex.com

"FINER WOEMANHOOD...."

FINE a WOMAN, *'hood...*

About "D" Author

"Arthur Miss(es) "Jane" Pit M(o)an...."

About "2" Book

*"No Body is going to CLAIM/BLAME Y-O-U
for doing What's "B" (W)right....")!?*

Dead-"D"-Cated

"2 ALL of Life's Love-Some Statuettes (of Liberties)'"

Explaining/Disclaiming <u>"pro bono/quid pro quo"</u>: "WE WHO HAVE NOTHING! Must do ANYTHING and EVERYTHING for "NOTHING"!! WE just(ly) want a LITTLE SOMETHING in terms of: COMPENSATION COMMENSURATE WITH OUR UNDYING EFFORT, RESULTING IN PUNITIVE AND CONSEQUENTIAL DAMAGES, from THIS LIFE Co-Conspirators/Prospective Cellmate(d), along with "Others" That may seek Asylum in The Suspect(ed)/Witness(ed) UnProtected LOVE PROGRAM ...."

—(Almost Anyone Who Never Volunteers
To Sell That Which They Cannot Give-Away)

ACTING ONE

"When The !st of You *Get- it-Up* There (to Heaven),
Don't You Go *Forking* Around With THAT Got Damn(ed)
"NYMS Family" ("Acronym;" "Antonym;" "Homonym;"
"Synonym;" "M" 'and' "NYMN;" "Pseudonym;"....)

"PREGNANCY PROTECTION"

WE(,) The NYMS(,) Family

EYE can "HEAR" the Dea(d) LION C(l)ub

Dystychiphobia "ROAR" ("W(H)INE")....

(E)WE "HERE"?!

Rebuke Not The Ones Who Know Not *("Knock-King-Knock")*

"If" you are the *"CLue,"*
Then I am the *"CLAN."*
To who (or "of WHOM")
You build the "clux" on *quick deed* Land...
Of an unkindled "boy-child, Crazy man"?!
When internity calls,
"The Soulless" are of a drunk and dried-out brand,
Unlike its *NEED* to be watered -
Living Within The Wholeness of Yet Another forever...
UNKNOWING but KNOWINGLY clever....

Degree!? *((E)WE "B" kidding me' KNEE(s))!?Rehearse(d) (or, "The cardiacs get to ride the CADILLAC!...pray it'll be good on the gas(ses)....)*

WE want forever to get yo' ride on heaven's LAMBORGHINI....
B! C(l)ause US's be onlookers for *THE Caddy-Act Peepers*....
                    (blue balls in a black (w)hole)

DisAgreeables!? *((E)WE "B" kidding me' KNEE(s))!?*

In accounting for DEGREES,
YOU better get Y-O-U a *CPA:*
CHILD PROTECTION ARK!!!

Echo:
my KIDNEY is stoned…..(follow(ed) me here: …then pass the stone and put that goat (KID(d) on your KNEE…(STAY(s) pissy drunk, lover)

So, This is Why Our Faces Are ALL Over The Baker's Dozen Milk Carto(o)n

"*The little FAT COW ate ALL of The BIG grass...
Then went looking for small(er) GRASS, and LOTS ....*"
("*WE LOVE(d) EWE, masseuse GRASSHOPPER*")

Rainbow Tear Chasing (2-Thawed-up)

Not awaiting the clouds to say,
"Whew!"
(if I didn't kiss back,
Don't be blue.)
Then, stir your own pot of gold,
Chase your dreams,
By *un-thawing* YOUR *"Behold."*

A Unkept Secret

Where did you keep your secrets?
Do you make them? Let's not tell?
Where did you bury a dead secret,
While drowning life in *YOUR* well?

Duplicity or Duplicate, But Not Replicate

"Replicate!" "Replicate!" "Replicate!"
Never get mad at the way a N-word,
Beg-N!.
The exact same difference as before,
NEXT time a BEGGING-knee-grower
Be stripped and searched at the *Dow* (*dough*).

VENGEANCE IS (Y)OUR SAID THE L(O)(A)RD

US WANT NO VENGEANCE!
WE WANT *REVENGEANCE!*

THANKS FOR THE FISH FRY!

LEST THE EAGLES FEAST!
WE'LL EAT COLD TURKEY!

I Begged to Do it ("The Difference")

One day (oh, by the way, it will be long coming),
But just keep being gone.
(Saying again, what *about* to say:
One day,
Somebody's wrong 2 take one of them props,
And miss hitting you on your propped-up-head.
Sitting up looking down in your own coffin like
Ain't the least bit caring to raise up: *You DEAD!?*

Why Blame The Puddle for Sipping on The Slippings?

Why blame the flood for his dry THIRST,
While WALKING to heaven underground?
The LAST shall drink the deserted FIRST,
Life SLIPS on WATER that is DROWNED.

Love, Respect, and Understand

I just want to roam like a lazy Free.
Respect Love's FIRST- in JAMMIN'
And LAST to integrate *a shammin'!*

How Many Pitchers of Tears in One's Death?
(*Whosoever Shall Have Ever* Worketh it in for You)

We both so dumb,
We resemble
The workers
Whose work's done
For the free.
Cause You and Yours
And Y'all Dummy,
Can't see,
And the *althoughs* WE
Might not, dare....
Cannot, so deadly, hear,
Are here.,
But You, definitively,
Do not sniff or smell.
Whoever works for you,
Must drink (from) under the table,
A cup of Death's death well....

Why Must The Soul Dehydrate for One Drop of Rain?

This rain soothes not *a pain*.
This rain rains like rain rains,
Leaving trails of blood stains.
Rain has no tempered refrain.
This rain is the drought's gain.
Leaving drought to thirst *Rain*.

You Shall Pay Attention Next Time

I did not know that we are so close
To the last end!
I did not know that nobody else know,
Do not pretend!

Moses, Did You Free Harriet? Harriet, Did They Get Stoned as a Well?

Your water has walked,
Who shouldn't WE do?
Let my peepers know!?
I pray you didn't mean,
MARK-SET-GONE-GO.

Lets Both Birds Open Fly

Both are Black Birds!
But WE eager to put
US in its *JAIL CELL*....

Thesis

Boy, you'll be better *wakeNup*.
Your bag ain't even fever filled.
Though tasted water in a CUP,
These's my evergreenery *years*....

WE Black Devils' US

Why giveth me a standing ovation,
Then maketh me crawl to the back?
Without any further risk to elevation,
I hate being Your love's devils' *black*.

I Just Pray That It Doesn't Rain Fowl During The Next Rain, Dear

My hoe, My Hoe, My hoe!!!
When Love is left to wander alone,
Which *ways* doesn't a trick go?
Your tow, Your tow, *Yo' tow*:
All the way down to the *wishbone*....

Hear Not the Fowl's Smell

I want fried chicken,
And I want chicken,
Fried.
Want to see *The* love!?
And a Love I can't see:
Cried...

Don't Play *The Dozen*

You look like you could be criminalized,
ALONE, with YOUR *Disciple-Nary-ACT*.
SITTING at the TABLE OF INJUSTICE,
The Baker's DOZEN uses *Silver Extract*.

Walk With Me to the Bank of Jordan, After Finding Your *Grand-Daddy* (Again) Records

Where your poured-over water Bank,
Bring with you Your *fishers and Sank*
Along the *Most* crowded road of Load.
Calling Your heavenly hand! *Do unfold.*

Not That You Are Not on The *UP on it*

WE do soooo MUCH,
BURE Sore Easy Fail...
YOU do so much of *it*,
YOUR *head* SWELL!

If The SUN Could Nurse Its Rhyming *Homophones*

Let me in, My COLDER Friend,
It is almost supper-setting-time.
Like a *Coup-Coup-Coup* Clock,
YOU just *WIND! WIND! WIND!*

Get on the UP, BIG SNOOZER,
You're on the stop-N-wait clock.
But WE are on OUR last bottled
Of *drop-off WINE! WINE! WINE!*

Your Mirror is Not The Imposter

The mirror is not Your imposter,
Will always showcase the faces
Aglow.
The mirror is not Your imposter,
The Mirror stare until Your eyes
Know....

GARDEN? TOOL! YOU AIN'T YET DRUNK? AFTER ALL US DONE-DONE TO SILVER-UP FAR US, *(Garden Tool)*

Today, I drink from the Well's Water!
I'll be smelling Their ASS tomorrow.
Tomorrow, *the waters* do flood Well.
"*CAIN*" See but, too Urn-able 2tale.

TEAR-TEARS-TEARY

"IF I COULD TEAR AWAY A TEAR,
WOULD TEAR A TEAR IN TEARS,
BEFORE BECOMING EYE TEARY....?

That Mule Would Not Have/HaveNot Abandoned US

WE legally blind,
Not one of Y'all!!
Riding SADDLE?
BUCK, Your FALL....

Not Today, Rain! Cleaning My Eyes For My *Pitcher (picture?)* of New Years Tears

For YOU who so Love(d) this world,
God is saving some of YOUR Tears...
For BROKE(n), *"MIRRORING Years"!!!*

Heaven Want(ed) You To Know/He(')ll Will Not Be Held Accountable"

Nigger #1: *Where are you going, Nigger Number One?* "I don't know" (very interesting question coming from *The Number One Nigger....*)

Nigger #2: Oh, dumb ass(ed) FOOL, In front of AND Behind The Trigger-Nigger, where do you wish NOT to go?....."Without KNOWING, someplace where...*where DEATH isn't SNOWING.*

What The Galaxy AND The Universe Both Said (Simultaneously)
To "The World"

"Child (but old enough to be a drunk),
Do You Want The World To See Your
milky wayyyyyy?"

Reporting for The UnRanked

Private?! *"SIMPLETON...."!,,,Reporting For "DO" "DO," Detail(ed)....*

M-Y Umbrella (*A poem for the Great, Late Whether Man/Woe-Man*)

Lord,

YOU (only) may borrow(ed) M-Y *Umbrella*...
("And, Y-O-U better not get 'ME" all WET!!")

Eye(?) See Fatty's PHAT (Hiding Behind The Woe-Man)

YOU so GODDAMN 'FAT" (" front and back"),
CAN see NOTHING "butt" YOUR lazy-ass-"I"!!!

***I**f We Were Your God(s)*

WE Would've Already Been The Magnificent Omnipotent

With a LOVE to absorb the BLOW of Humanity's *PUNCH*....
With all *The Bread(D)* take(N) from The Water(ed), *Late LUNCH*....

Re-See-Cup

"Your Blood is on My Life"

"My Life is on Your Blood"

BROKE(N) WORD, EVEN

"I WILL TAKE ALL YOU GOT FOR GIVING ME ALL THAT I GET WHEN GOT(TEN)!!!???)"

THERE IS BUT ONE WAY TO GET (T)HERE

FUCK THAT "ONE WAY ROAD BULLSHIT"!
WE TOOK THE STRAIGHT AND NARROW...
AND FOOLS HEAR WE HERE: "S(W)(EAR)"!?

WE LIKE WHAT WE LIKE WE LIKE IT....
("MONEY" TO THE LIKE(R))

I LIKE WHAT YOU LIKE.
YOU LIKE WHAT I LIKE.
"LIKE WHAT WE LIKE"?
"US LIKE WHAT WE LIKE,,,,,,"?!

If I AM Not Perfect For You....

*Then, I PRAY That I'm PERFECT(ED)
FOR MY "NEXT" PERFECTIONAL(S)....*

(E)YE' Charge The Juror With Executing The Execution(ER)

"EYE Will Charge GOD With Crime,
Before I Let MY Brother "MOTHER
SUCKER" Set ME UP for F(l)(r)ee...."

Deal, Dough

US Just Love (Y)OUR LOVE for THE big-LITTLE guy:
"SUCK(ED) AFRICA 'AND' NOW FUCK(ED) Dead-DRY...."

BROKE(N)WORD

MY LIFE SPENT ALL OF MY TIME *GETTING IT ON DOWN*,
NOW THIS DEATH IS DARING ME *TO GET IT BACK ON UP...*
(WITHOUT FROWN)?!

BLACK EYE SORE(S)

"WE WILL FEEL MUCH BETTER ABOUT OVERCOMING WHEN WE GET IN TOUCH WITH THE HEAD"

("WITHOUT US TOUCHING US ON THE HEAD WE WOULD THINK BETTER ABOUT OVERCOMING")

ImPloyed

Whether *Job* or Job,
Or Job or Job,
We are im-ployed.
Should the hot-watered
Need to grow mold?
Let *death* catch its "weller":
One-Flood-Hoard....

I Really Don't NO Ewe

I don't Truly know YOU!
Love is sheepish TOO!!
Before I *de-grace* a ewe,
I'd die walk-N from hue!!!

Cometh Comet Come (The Lead Layer of Thee Led 2 Lead)

Of the twelve swell constellational signs,
Failing-Falling-Failed, (in *mine* eye),
All but US going back to heaven,
With their un- dying-weeper-baby, cry.
Star, Star, Star,
Having landed on dirt's-dusty-mound,
Why must your overflowing give watered-tears to
Your drowned-out-under-*the-grounds?*
Why must Life *be-gone-lost*, searching for
The Missing?
Where must The "N" begin thy TRUTH,
Complictly-Competing-Like Competition?
That dim-wit-half LIT,
At the bar, blessing-the-god-damned dead, SAID:
"Follow Not-Dim-Knot-Night,
If not from yo' Knotty-Head
That seduces their LOVERS,
While carrying them unto HISS'
JAIL, in death's hot-hell-held-hailed-handle-basket,
And didn't "we" ("again") No? *N-JUST-ICE* is chillin',
Firing off cheap shots to the sleepers in
D(I)E-LEAD-BED!!!

Where....
(*Gonna Go Gone*)

I know where My Love has gone!:
"Wrong"?!
Too many old JOKERS in my *KNEW*
Deck of Cards...
Done!?
Traded a chariot that couldn't take me to heaven
For the doe ("dough") that not just any
Love-Lusted-Jezebel can cut bait,
After hook-N but un-reeling-on
These-They-Like-Thee-Light-Days,
In the Darkest-Knight of The Shark!!!

Whaling-*Wailing-Welling*

Sore-Sew-So,
I carry my tow!
You walk slow...
"Stub Yo' Toe"!

Did You *Spell* My Shame Wrong?

I Don't Know What You DoNot Know,
That You Know Not What I DO Know.
But If I Were Your Teacher, You'd *BE*
Promoted for Believing N-word:*SLOW*....

Just Be Somebody Else's Jive, Cool?

If you've stolen the Talents and don't mis-use,
Someone is going to remain *con-crossed-ruse*....

The Redeemables Down Down Here

If not for the lifelessness Life gave freely
To the Lifeless,
We would not have been left here....
That death will come crawling with its back to me,
This redemption,
Must I not fear?

Don't Want No More Life To Arrive un-urn-Alive!

Don't Want No More Life and To Arrive un-urn-Alive!
Last breath of the everlasting *LIFE* shall never outLAST,
Don't Want No More Life and To Arrive un-urn-Alive!
BE genuinely happy for LOVE coming home a' *LAST*....

DYING TO DIE WHEN ALREADY DEAD FROM DYING

"AT LAST YOU HAVE ARRIVED LAST AT LAST; DEAD COME HERE *FAST TO BE LAST*"

"WE'VE BEEN GOING TO THE GRAVE TOO FAST TO LAST PAST DYING DEAD LAST"

"DID YOU LEAVE ANY CLOWNS BEHIND TO LAUGH AT THE LAST OF THE LAUGHING DEITIES (TAKING JOKES AT THEY OW(N) WORD *WORD*)"

"WE HAVE RUN OUT OF "(K)NEW "DO" "DO" FO(O)D, MAY WE BOIL UP LAUGHING GAS JUST FOR YOU"?!

"I Swim(MED) TH(ROUGH) Three Shining "Cs" To Play "Crazy See(S)...."

"SO(RE)(')-Crazy"

"DEBIT (left alone) and/both C(RED)IT"?!...Do (E)WE have another... "CHILD(RE)(N)" "Word" "CARD"?!

WEPERFECTSTORM(S)!!!: "EWEHURRY(CANE)" "USTORN!?.... NAY, DOUGH!!!

"Your 'DNA' Didn't Beget Love, 'DANA'"

"NO BODY got the goddamn right to complain..."
"EVERY BODY" dies so LIFE must be sustained....

"Richard" HEADS ("D" "baker(s) do(zen)")

"PEOPLE! EWE "MAY" (the "month") STOP (SPEA(K)ING) IN COD(E)(D) TONGUES...BECAUSE (Y)OUR INTERPRETERS TAUGHT "Y'ALL" ("ALL OF US") THE LAN(G(U)A(U)GE) ("12 in the barrel, one in the 'hold-stir'....")

"D" SWEET(EST) SUPERLATIVES WE ALL DID DONATE(d)

"LOVE,

MAYBE WE SHOULD CALL YOU - 'DO' 'DO' DOWN MOLASSES, (B)! BECAUSE YOU GET ON OUR LAST SET OF (U)(P)ASS(ES)"

"THE name is "Miss(il(l)(e) American Piper"!...and "peter,"
You might WANNA (this "time")
PAY PICK(LED) P(C)IPER....

ACTING TWO

"SOMEBODY TO LOVE? *or, SOMEBODY* TO LOVE ME?"

The Confectioners Sugar IS Sweet(T)est

"AIN'T NO DADDY LIKE A SUGAR DADDY, CAUSE SUGAR POURS IN RAIN AND WALK/TALK WITH THE SWEETEST SUGAR CANE"

AIN'T NO LOVE LIKE DEAD LOVE, CAUSE DEAD LOVE DIED DEFYING LOVE'S PAIN AND SHALL (WILL) NEVER DIE DEAD AGAIN"

LOVE, HOW MAY I HELP YOU TO HELP ME TO LOVE ME LIKE LOVE IS THE LOVE OF MY LOVE?

"RUN AWAY WITH LOVE AND HELP LOVE TO HELP THEE LIFE FLEE"

"MÉNAGE À TROIS" ("3X3X3X....")

THE NIGGERS ON MY BACK AND THE **bLACKS** ON THE FRONT, GONNA HAVE A MENAGE A TROIS....LIFE BEING A DEAD CUNT!

THE LOVE OF YOUR LOVE LIFE HAS BEEN PHOTOSHOPPING ("RE-LYING" ON DEATH)

"THAT DON'T EVEN LOOK LIKE US!?...ANYWAY(S) WE LOVE THE OTHER PICTURE OF US, WHEN WE WERE NOT DEAD.... WE(')LL MAK(D)E-UP US

UP TO LOOK LIKE WE ARE THE LOW DOWN(ES)...."

EYE SEE(,) bLACK NUMB(BERs) "n" "d" D(ARK)

LOVE,
"I AM YOUR *'H-E-R-O'!* 'U..r...MY("my")...
'H-E-R-O-I-N' (*"Her(r)-Run"*)"

Little Child's Weep (If "not" for" "teething" "RICH AND UGLY" "Babies Cry")

Roses and throngs and lovers' meaningless flings,
Once meant nothing but now doesn't mean a thing.
You kiss with a child's wisdom, holding *The tongue.*
                ALWAYS...
Holding back that tongue...(otherwise too old to be acting
ALL amish-like-YOUNG)...
When you come back home, WE shall still be waiting!
I say "we" with little more than an unexpected Re-cleansing,
                WATCHING...WASHING....
Wasn't the first to chase LOVE until love never ended....,
That LOVE *aren't* the SAME-FOR-ONE who gets to relive the UNLIVABLE-
                AGAIN...
Weep MY little BIG...*JAILing-BOY-BABY.*
Weep with *US* as *YOU* lead the black sheep through hell to make HEAVEN-
                JUST*(us)!?*
(coming back for hell's own d*usty-D-dust?!*)
Dead Flowers and funerals...all you ever consummate...overflowing, U
                ABUNDANTLY GIVE.
If a cunt can never (*bleep*)- "A-child,"
Was NOT heaven also complicit when Y'ALL
                N-ed this-deal?!

ONCE A DOG....

*"ONCE THE BARK HAS BEEN ROOFED,
LOVE BITES ARE MITIGATED RUFFED"!?*

After Love Kicked Their Own(er) Bucket

Love kicked those fools' buckets!
(No not that life do commandeer)
But before love kicks *The Bucket,*
Let's Love US like a Buck is Dear....

"Merry, Is 'XMAS' Okay?!

WE Forgive US, *Love*
For not promoting OUR own
BEAUTY products,
But darkness in any other-green-colors
Isn't "A" *STILL* (or "steal").
The most BEAUTIFUL name for someone who
Looks foolish in ALL of *they* (or "day")
Black-ash-ness just trying to be "hue-man" (or "been" human....)?!

("THE SANDY CLAWS
GOT FUCKIN' LOST,
WHILE DES(S)ERTING
THE "NORTH POLE(s)!
("THIS CAT'S (C)OLD")
BUT, WAITING ON LOVE
ISN'T UNLIKE DROWNING
IN THE PATIENCE of BLACK...
    (HOLE!?, or HOLD?!)"

Which of The Darker Nights Not Already Promise(d) 2 Another Day

Today is NOT the Last day for a *Love-Away*,
Cause the Last Day for this is *"NOT Today"!!!*

Punish Me My Butchering/Bastard

What did WE not get right this time,
Pretentious Love,
On hiatus,
Just to come crawling back,
On "3N1" day?
If LOVE is betting on getting something
Other than LIFE's other misgivings,
I'd just ABRUPTLY stop
Whatever I'm not doing...
AND restart livin'....

Aches Incurable

Now!!!
U Talking UNDERSTANDING2!?
LOVE speaks in holey "BRAILLE,"
A life never ever fully delivered is
Urn-Like, a "internalized" forgiver,
Living/Dying in my own *LITTLE*
"Jail Cell"....

If I Were to Enter Unto The King's Pen

I would not permit the wolf to partake ("parlay")
With its flocks servings being served abundantly,
Underneath chicken-infested-tables of emptiness,
I'd rather spend long-tithing-time getting Heaven –
"Address(ed)....".

Miss Who!

Miss Who?
Do I look like a man to you?
Miss who?
(Baby Daddy Dark-N-BLUE)!!!

Redemption To Salvation

I am truly terrified,
Of the one who delivered me from *MY terrification*:
A belief in education.
The innocent heart does not implicate.
Like with any duel with love,
Salvation is its own forgiver.

When Voices Begin to Echo

Whether you jumped in,
Fell in, slipped in,
AND still cannot get out,
Can make fate wonder,
If hope dies not exhausted,
But LAST clout is in doubt....

Entrapment

Best saved some of those tears for heaven.
Heaven settles for time's entrapped resolve.
Save some of the years for twelfth of eleven,
Forever won't be cheated out of love's brawls.
Sometimes it's unclear if heaven *Aborts Time*,
Or just breaks a glass heart to pieces to Glee.
Based on un-fundamental fairness of a rhyme,
Love whispers songs until *whisperings* go flee....

Dance Baby Dance

On the floor,
We can make romance.
Dance Baby Dance
Give ourselves a Tango of a chance.
Dance Baby Dance
Make your half-dollar
Bring home a *grand*.
Dance Baby Dance
Find yourselves in a romantic band.

I Haven't Been Kicked Out of a Better Heart Than Mine

I haven't been kicked out of a better heart than mine,
And there is still something worse than a heart crying.
After I had broken out of the loneliness that is all real,
Emphasized with love and forgot to forget and forgive.

Now This is Convalescing

You are mine,
Because I belong to you.
When you are hollow,
I am empty, too.
Because I belong to you,
Can we shower (recover)
In this fountain of *dew*?

BRIDE(D) AND GROOM(ED)

TRUE LOVE IS ITS OWN OWNERS BRIDE AND GROOM,
THE BED IS NOT DEFILED, GIVEN BREATHING ROOM!!

Abomination

Abomination:
What we must never *Do*,
When it's just the US too.

Abomination:
Climaxing in the fiery Hell,
Ice drop from drunks-Well.

Abomination:
The price WE must now pay
To be grinning at *Latter theys*....

Expecting Again (or "Stay With Me Until Forever Hook Up With Eternity")

I could have told you
Today isn't tomorrow,
And you will still pray
That yesterday *stays*
In a Family-Like-Way.

"LOVE IS A DOGGONE BULLY"

"LOVE IS A SICK, DOGGONE BULLY, CHICKEN BONE WITHOUT PULLEY"

LAST FAST OF LOVE

(OF LOVE, LOVE WILL FAST AT LAST):

THE BIGGEST FOOL LOVE IS FULL OF
KEEPS YOU STUCK IN THE MIDDLE OF....
DEAD LASTS TOO LONG TO NOT LAST,
DO NOT WE DIE LOVE DEATH AT LAST....
LOVE IS OUR FUTURE PAST THAT FAST,
LOVE TAKE BACK THE TIME DEAD FAST....

Take Over for Me (At Your Breaking Point)

Take over for US, and let The "US" KNOW:
With OUR *"WE" "WE,"* WE Piss Fo' SHOW!
Take over for US then KISS WHILE DOWN –
LIFE's LAST DIVERSION, *breakin' FROWN*....

AND or (Looking Back Into The Mirror
AND or Not Been Recognized....)

While looking at the mirror and not recognizing myself....
AND I am finally leaving, or
Haven't I been left!?

EITHER LOVE ME OR KILL THE LOVE IN ME FOR LOVE

WHY MUST THE CHILDREN PAY THE PIPER FOR THEIR PIPERING?
MUST THE DEAD CRY OUT TO DEATH WITH THE DYING SCREAM?

ACTING THREE

*"WE DON'T WANT (Y)OUR CHILDREN GROWING
UP FEELING ASHAMED OF US"*

(H)OUR

WE are borne to SHIT, And Then Die From ITS SORROW;
WE await Our Hour With Death, From Time We BORROW......

P-D-N-R (Peace Does Not Rest)

Peace never does take a rest.
Live a while and take the test.
For all of your earthly sorrow,
ONE's consolation is P-D-N-R....

A Bounty on Your Beauty

Your beauty is the eyes that un-shames my soul.
And, of course, my love is very appreciative of this.
If the journey to paradise is rose pedaled with gold,
Then love has granted the open-hearted "the" wish.
You are the unparalleled companion who flaunts life
Between virtuous beauty and its Comely Endeavor.
You are the reflection of a Merciful waiting in TRUST,
Reaching arms out to the owners of the *sown LUST!*

JUST SEEDLESS

I'M JUST THE SEEDS THAT FEED THE WEED KILLERS GREED....
I'M JUST THE SEEDS THAT INDEED BEGAT THE *DEAD BREED*....

IT'S ME(,) *JOB*

GOT LOTS
OF PLOTS!
DEAD GOT
LOTS FULL
OF PLOTS -
(?dashings?)

NIGHT IN A *THEY* LABOR CAMP

HOW DEEP IS THE DEPTH OF THE DARKNESS?
PLENTY IS THE BREAD TO BE EATEN IN LIGHT?
SO THE DEAD-RIDDEN MUST OFTEN CONFESS:
DARKEST BLUES ARE EVEN DARKER AT NIGHT....!

You Too Never Sleepy For Me

Can't be sleeping on my *THEY* job,
Cannot be awake while passed out.
This song's just another wishful Star,
Wishing that Night didn't have clout.

HUMMIN' HYMNS

AS LONG AS YOU ARE BLACK,
LIVING IN THIS DARK AMERICA,
YOU'VE *"PSEUDONYMed"* LIFE...

INTO THE DARKNESS THE LIGHT BURN O(W)N....

OUR GAS AND 'ELECTRIC
WERE NOT TURNED OFF -
(LAUGHING GAS BURN ON)....

WHILE WE MAY NOT SLEEP

WHILE *US* MAY NOT SLEEP,
WE GOT DREAMS TO KEEP!

The Untimely Must Settle With Time

May the sun set on love leave the lovely star that you are....
May time never take away time when taking time to LOVE....
Thine OWN star....

KILLER O' JOY

WHEN THE RAINS CRY TEARS,
RAIN WANTED YOU TO KNOW
THE TEARS IN *RAINED* YEARS.
RAIN ALSO CRIES TEARS FOR
KILLERS O' PRECIPITATED JOY...

Just Like "ME"

If You Don't Do Any Better Than "ME,"
Love Wants You To *JUST LIKE "M-E"*!

GOD's GUARDS ARE MY WITNESS(ES) ("Back-Up (K)now(s)

"NIGGERS Always (start) (taking) *"THE SHIT(S)*...
For "butterflies"!? Give those *blacks CONSTIPATION*....

The God in Me Does Not Want To Lose/Win The Fight With The God in Me

"I will NOT *look for God* until God gets the vision to STOP me from not being able to tell LITTLE dusty black *lies* from BIG dirty White *liars*, Cause when sweeping Heaven's Park(N) Lots, Hell's bottom shelf is ALL Rainbow(ed) UP in its *BLUE DIE*"!

ACTING FOUR

"WE MUST TAKE BACK HEAT THAT SHIELDS US FROM THE SUN"

GOD is MY Witness ("Back UP" (K)now!)

US Niggers Start(ed) *THE SHITS,*
So(re') WE Get *(T)Heir('s) CONSTIPATION!!!*

Whether Prosecuted or Weather Persecuted....
(Life Didn't See No Body from "Justice")

Whether LOVE prosecuted ME,
or,
Weather LOVE persecuted ME,

(WE The *"5ᵗʰ TAKERS"* take ASSAULT in KIND, 47 WAYS....)

Why can't Death Be *"JUST US"* TONIGHT,
And *WE be* "OUR" "KILLERS" "BEST theys"?!

"YOU" Mis(s) Spell(ed) "freedom"

"FREEDOM" is *spelled* with 'a' *uppercase* 'F,'*YOU"!!!*

TROUBLES DOUBLE FOR DOUBLE TROUBLE

G(R)AVE The Children' Milk to the "BABIES"!!
NOW! Let LOVE Labor in Dead-Death-PAIN!!!
Coming Back Home with All of The "MAYBEs,
Leaves YOUR BLOOD a COMPLICIT STAIN....

When UR Person #5 in Your Mirror Lying-UP —

"Given the "Statutory Limitation" of The Selection Process Itself, The Mirror (which, incidentally does not LIE), has purposefully reciprocated on The Witness that petty crime(s) is/are for pettier criminals. Being an Offender to REPEAT, most of LIFE is PREDICATED on the premise that One does not PRECIPITATE THEIR O(W)N DEATH....*(Prayerfully...4 reel, dough))*, GOD RECITATION GIVE "LIFE "tea"...(..."WHEN YO' DEATH CAUGHT YOU PLAYING WITH GOD'S ID(EA)(L)...

("THE TRUE LOVE(R)(S) of 'Life' PLEA(D) 4 "THE FIFTH")....

YOU ARE JUST MY 'Just' Cup of 'COFFEE' ("rain dear"!!!)

WE BOUGHT FROM US TWO (2) CUPS OF COLDWATER COFFEE, VERY HOT....!
WE SLEEP WITH INSOMNIA AND DREAM OF TAKING LESS THAN HATE GOT....!

I Found The Perfect "GEM" 4 MY (Be)Love(d)...

I opened MY Heart and answered, *What Matters Love The Least at Most?* "When *slicing bread*, Love's BUT(T)ER) making slippery - ITS TOAST..."

or,

To TRULY Reciprocate(d) Love, feelings must FILL what feelings FEEL... "Love seesaw "Diamonds in Its Eyes, When TREADING At The Mill(ER)..."

Going to The Bank (...*AND Gonna Drown Your Blood in My Blood, Money*)

or,

*Another Way 2 Screw EWE at The Drownings for **J**ordan's **R**iver:*

I'm riding a *"Chariot,"* carrying a "caravan" of - NIGGERS!!! Some Shiver but most Crank, but ALL get "Jacked" on *The Way 2 "D" River Bank*... ...Never seen so much WATER flooding AT *THE New Niggs' Bank!* Going ahead of Y-O-U!? *"Know you Ain't*...I'se been banking on "J's" BANK (not going bankrupt 'til...let's just see what they say when they *here* WE HERD......" Going to the Bank, AND break one make a loan 'against ONE fool soul in name only, FOOL ("did your little CAPITALISM sit in, in the inn, N? If you weren't a fish, they'd have to make you a new set of "The FINs"!....Anyway (child), "I saw that fish first"! "I bet that you better not dirt-up another one of my blouses AND bring them back clean." ("Individual #1...EWE so MEAN")!? ("guessing WE DO...US must propose...)...."Any Way U-Go (not *the* "CAR" again) I go, if you CAN go..." Do you want a fish, or do you want to fish?" There is a difference and here lies the least of The LIEs THE Least Lie(s) About: "Love(s)(ed) me some of THAT *Chattahoochee (B)ass* ("mullet") "Praise The *Sewers* (They *"sew"* you, so you should *"sore"* 'em Back....(Watch the next *Catfish Be BLACK?*)....("I love me some Niggers but Niggers don't always show love foe M-E! Just because I told a once blind nigger: "FOOL, you better be looking, since you can't *SEE* (...AND The Sanks said: "I see what you saw. You saw what I see"(wish ALL the bitches would AGREE not to DISAGREE...)...("There's a difference between what YOU cook, AND MY eating what I like — since WE ain't ALL married AND don't ALL claim the *SAME - child*, (gonna sit this BOTTLE on THE table for *A WHILE*... ("Patient, MY Love" ("Pigeon Dove")...*("eagles devour pistol(less) stoolcarringPIGEONS, AND hearThey are The-Diss-US, 2")*... Get you behind ME, SUN TAN(ed)...Who do I fear? I FEAR "fear." I'm FULL of FEAR! When I was *the child*, and did what I was TOLD! They said, "Be fear...full").... So, I says to big FEAR!: "FEAR ain't nothing but falling backwards while *Cryng* to crawl forward...) At least this is what US is scared of: "WE, THE SHITS make 'em *"DO"/"DO"*...at THE BANK of(for) That NAKED-GIRL's OUTHOUSE(es).....

"JAIL AND HELL" ("CHICKEN")

*AFTER SUN DAY SCHOOL,
LYING DEAD AT SERVICE...*

MISTAKELESS

IF YOU'RE MY ONLY LIFE,
YOU ARE DEATH OF ME?
WHY SHOULD LOVE RUN,
WHEN LOVE CAN'T FLEE?
IF LOVE IS THE ANSWER,
LOVE DOES HATE HATE!!!
DOES DEATH KILL *A LONE,*
KILLING LOVE'S MISTAKE?!

Leap(T)

"If I could spend but ONE day with you,
I PRAY only that it is the last LEAP Yr."

"FINER WOMANHOOD...."

FINE a (W)O(E)-ME(A)N, ' **hood...**

WE MUST MAKE US SPEAK IN OUR TONGUES

*(I speak their languishes: WELL-DEEP)....**echo....**)*

I speak their bilingual, barbaric *LANGUAGE*....
But my dialect isn't always crystal clear...
I can see the caboose trains' *a cumming,*
While sleeping on death's tracks...*I hear*...

I speak their languishes,
And I've spoken MY languages as(s) I don't sleep...
There is no hole in THE soul
That runneth more DEEP!!!

I speak death's languages,
And This tongue that I speak is
ONE Tongue that FREEDOM speaks:
There are NO lamenting LANGUAGES/LANGUISHES
That wouldn't DARE drown **a LITTLE river that ran *WELL* into its....
DEEP!!!**

Do You Want *"A"* Rock? or, Do You Need *"C"* Rock To Help Rock You Off And Away To Your Rock***(ER)*? ? ?**

She said, "I'm tired of This Cohabitation With MY *Bottle(d) UP SIN*, *Wanna* 'Rock'! before *My Time* has no more time to untimely *LEND* ...."
He said, "All I want is a *LITTLE peace* that I can call *ALL OF MIND*. Gonna *'Re-Fire and Re-Load,'* Then waste MIS(S)calculated *TIME* ...."

You Too Never Sleepy To/For Me

Can't be sleeping on the *theys' Job*,
Cannot be awake while passed out.
The Sun's just another wishing *Star*,
Wishing that *Night* didn't have clout.

Who Can't Dream of Love During These Good Night Times?

Who can't dream of love,
When warming up to the night's timeRs?
        After this?:
I just lost My will to be the Kissed,
My lips did die awaiting your heart.
Now, Love's resuscitated Breath's
A New Life of Kissed-Off reWards!?

Owned Ashes

I haven't been talking about US,
Not behind OUR *backs*!
Although WE did buy *Love*,
Lots of slacks.
"WE are US,"
So the US must be composed of ALL of the US.
No more of THE lonely ONE going *clubbing*,
Not in a FREEDOM-NAMED-LAND!
Storied on riches from the underdown rotten Man.
Neither will a freedom be fermented from the crust of ill-dated bread,
Frowning at the taste of a maligned *Peoples* mixing,
Forgetting that a diamond is a diamond,
      Whether polished or not....
In fact, "Should WE Shall Not Forgot:":
The most beautiful diamonds were placed on a broken,
        MIDDLE FINGER
That YOU Raised up to The *ALL Mighty* for All,
After burying YOUR *owned* ashes above **THE thorny lots....**

My Water Drips Like The Breakings of Broken Gripes

If I was making love to my *bitches*,
I couldn't get as hard up as a deadless,
Dick,
Suffering from uncontrollable pissing,
Flooding the lowly with an open palm
To finance their begging to be loved.
I will hold on to my motivators,
Though you'd still buy your own death,
(Which isn't easy to sell).
I am going to piss US a lil' bit' harder,
And pray-hope that WE,
Being one of a kind with KOOL(aided) unique,
PUTS the freeze on hell.

So Melanin-Koilee of the SUN

Don't just YOU wait and try to then see,
After the sun's done and as(s) hot as *us,*
The SUN can be immature, likes to fuss.

Don't make the wait longer than *waiting!!!*
The SUN can get misty-eyed: *(favors US).*
The SUN can't right any wrongs, *as it lust.....*

The Locked Outs That Threw Away Their Keys (Players)

Why CALL my life, GOOD?.
Never hasn't been 'bout LIFE
That really is no good at living.
Since this latest Ruining Year,
Time is almost upping again,
Cause WE, US, ALL *Friends*.

What's it gonna take to take it
Back? Living in darkness, not
DisBelieving it fades to *black?*
We are One but one *Ain't US!!!*
Take it from the slower runners
Who still is running' bitterly slow....

The key to breaking a RUNNER is:
Making THIS "N" ("word") run more!?'.

The Giver

I have never taken a gift,
So, I must be the GIVER.
If Love were not a BABY,
Do you *STILL* DELIVER?

Collection Call

I'll take a plate up for you:
The dollared-down,
Disrobed.
Don't cheat Your Collectors,
They count the over time,
           Souls.
Can't cheat the other collector,
Neither,
Cause these collectors' Cheat(ed),
Mis Discounted the *WEEP(ER)s*.
Although ALL must lie in the BED,
US sheets can bleach an "N"-keep(er)!!!

Under the Stone, Hidden (Righting of Wrong)

Many a Peoples have come,
Then forever never gone.
Strip search eternity,
And do look under the hidden stone.
Discover the fate of thy truth,
The plight of freedom,
Traveling with the righting of wrong.

ALL of US is EQUALLY-QUALITY-FIED

WE SHALL NOT TAKE ANY of US with US.
YOU ARE GOING TO MISS *THIS FOOL*, *bus(T)*....

Reverse My Prayer

The things you prayed for me,
I, NOW, do not want...*EITHER*....
(Same distance between do/don't.)
The things I prayed blindly for,
Now, I *DON'T* from *a Y-O-U.*
But, tell us that you *DON'T* see.

If The SUN Were Gangster Like its Ring Kissers ("Let US Burn 'Em)

Why Do You Love Mister *SUN*?

"Because (after this, gonna *burn* the Lists)...
Because (again),
WE just love the US's SUN!
The SUN's been HOTTEST in *The US* (the *real* hot "us").
US just loves the SUN when it's *nigger-shining!*
The SUN rains and shines and still DELIVER,
Maintaining the SUMMER's time.
Shucks, the warmest sentiment Ever given,
On the backtracking of YOUR and MINE *(the sun, Sun & SUN)*.
Makes the boiled-down blood shriver,
Especially when the SUN gets uncontrollably,
HOT HEADED (but always a DIGGER),
Makes the candle lick the wit of The Heaters
QUICK TRIGGER...."

NOW, Why Don't YOU Love *US* Some, *SUN*?
(UNBURNT, NIGGER)!!!

Love is a Mute's-Mute-Muted

Speak now, Child,
Cause *DAY's* **done:**
KNOT talking to the US
Gently killed-D-WILL,
When dust is DIRTY
Death is TRUST!?!?!?....................(trust—a-GENT?)

Beau Tied *(These Theys of Mind)*

My days used to be long,
Like yours is a long short.
Truth was the longest too.
One day could be so long,
Before it wasn't even over,
I shall be *waiting,* **My** *BOO*....

SUN SUNNY SUNNIEST (NOT-NEVER-GONE!?)

If YOU are as bad as they said you ain't HOT,
Then blow me up with some of what you GOT.
(I already know ALL I *k(no)w* about the *w(h)ine*....)....
I want some of that *Nigger-get-the-hell o(w)n up* in my CUP.
        Just a Taste (*just a lit', bit'*)!
Before breaking into The House with my abundantly overflowing
EMPTY BOTTLES, FILLED TO THE TOP WITH TOO MUCH EMPTINESS....
(breaking in broken bottles)....
Real NIGGERS *knows* ("niggers is just an umbrella term(ed)....
(like **"PTSD"** is the umbrella "word" **FOR** "ptsd")
Rebottled Chicken Working like orgasmic *Gin*.
"Well" (don't fall into the wrong "wail"),
If you not as BAD as you ain't so HOT,
Why *doesn't* YOU never bluff-N no lot?
I've been drinking like a drunk on that drank,
To hydrate a dehydrated thirst for so LONG,
My little CHEAP bottle of Nile River
Ain't almost NOT-NEVER-GONE!?)

I'll Take The Usual Beat Down

Let me beam to the ground;
The ground KNOWS to LAY.
If Ground is drugged Right,
It's THE shadow of a DAY ("they"! Can't help 'em).

Job Ain't Not Nearly Finished! (*BossN, Everybody!?*)

WE IS NOT DONE WITH YOU $ US (big MONEY)....
(could've used one "period).
You're the left to a right, beaten shoe.
Give You Alms, but You want STEW.
WE have baked and cooked on OUR
        OWN!!!
YOU must become patient, *STRONG!*

*Take The Deal!..Take The Meal!!...Take The **HILL!!!***

I will give you the other ⅔ that was being subtracted
From the ⅗ that I DO still owe you FOR *workACTing*.
Not knowing the STRENGTH of YOUR MIGHTY *few*,
I WOULD NOT sleep on this deal, <u>*being*</u> *I GOT HUE (baby)*.

Nothing Goes to Waste in My Belly

In my belly I wasted My Bread.
THIS is the Movement I Dread.
Like wishing a CONSTIPATION
Grounded-up a *Liquored Nation*.
While LIFE also made its Mess,
NOBODYS 2 clean UP but *Rest*.

Knot Going To Tell You, Until After WE Been Consummated

"LUCK YOU" behind DBack.
If I didn't KNOWS me better,
Would not have sworn YOU
Don't BEAT not being Black.

How Many Cookies in One's Jar?

I ate so many fish eggs until I now hate Caviar.
Maybe the death of Life is in hell's *Cookie, JAR*.

I've Found *No Body*

Everybody is dying, *O'Lardy!*
Where's life's forgivable twin?
Should I find Love lit' bit' tardy,
Save me a cup of *Good SIN!!!*

Is The SUN Seriously This Hot?

Then come on back and stew in MY POT.
BOILS Me like its pack of Canned Goods.
Then, CUT off the taint that yielded a LOT,
After hiding a death up under those *Hoods*.

That *Mercy-Free* Cannot Count (The Last Word Rhymes With the Title EverLaughing Word....*UP*)

Forgive me for transgressingN:
If I am your everlasting *MULE*,
Then, Love, let their asses *diss* -
MOUNT!!!

Diss-Re-Covered
(For The Upper AND DOWNER Fool-Us-Un-Fooled (wait a minute).........
(They also swear they don't B getting Life's lows on high/lows on Hi Yo")

That Nigger is blessed,
Recovering *Ped-A-Pile.*
If WE were not our own,
Purified 2-dd-TRIGGER,
Love will steal B-2-Loud,
    "*My Hither.*"
("And Those Were "D" Theys")

Impossinay (*Whine* Not N-WORDed Up)

It is going to be impossible
For US to keep up,
With moving heaven again,
MOUNT-OF-MOUNTAINS OF SINS!
"Shall WE mount-10-Ns together?
Don't YOU! N-near-deadly, WE *strays* to the US?
NAY!!!"

When You Cannot Get a Date and Your Other Date
Shows Downer-AND-Upper

You will never (again) drug me with that blood ready wine.
You ain't gonna have me swinging like a fermented grape,
On that de-VINES.
Nope, *Dope!*
It's my HOPE
(GO VOTE!!!)
(Shall Not Love
Forever TOTE..........................!?

You Are Not Late Until After Your Blood Doesn't Come Sneaking Back Like a Run Down

What had happened after -
the next time that you re-use me again?
Will you put holy water in that hole, brother *GIN*?
Shall I follow the GAME of "scratch-off" with big *SIN*?
Do I lose my everlasting last place at the *Re-Tarders* table,
2 half-dozen (+1) pass the end of the starting gate?
Or will you come back for one everlasting last good time,
To kill the golden shovels for such a little HATE?
Life had to have known that love, too, runs into the well,
When chasing a virgin that only commingled with another lover,
While precipitating death, and starving in the barbed wire (bosom) of the deads' *JAIL*.
("To kill the golden shovels for such little HATE!?")
But daddy's boy isn't concerned about his image,
Out celebrating a redemptive period that's
So-unwed-lockedly LATE.

Rushing When Brushing

Love,
Why must I be smitten by the gold rush?
Death's too shiny, chasing-bronze- crush.

Your Only Ways!?

You may go,
But you must find your own way.
You may stop to rest,
If only for a night to renew its focus
On the none-ending, forever new day.
You must find,
And may never get to *KEEP*!
But You will Up the laugh
On House Money for cutting
Cornerstones into big pieces of dust,
Relatively speaking, Instantaneously, too,
Following love's grandiest *WEEP*.

Shouldn't Been Re-Written Away

Boy, I ain't re-dying behind no *re-lies*.
But, We do need a bit' lit' mo' support,
Since god did not *make children wise*,
Girl, that devil's truly hangin' *Lit'* short....

Always Getting Taken Taking The Shortcut (How Much Longer is My Forever Willing to Make Love an Urn-Waiter?)

How much longer forever?
Double dipping for eternity,
When we are not together.
How long is waiting to be?
Weight sucks the gallant in,
After you're dead and gone.
Does an attacked heart die?
Can it just deceive insomnia?
(Always seemingly awakeN.)
When life tow love and pull,
Isn't love now a row - lulled?

Take My Picture After The Wedding

Take my picture after the wedding,
See if I blush or cry!
Should death last longer than Life,
Pee if I fuss or Redie!?

TELL LOVE BEST STOP RELYING ON ME

LOVE *LOAN* YOU FREE**(LIE),**
THEN TAKE YOUR INTEREST:
"LET LOVE DREAM OF LOVE"

Love Me Under The Same Hot-Air-Conditions

Love me under love's unforgivable condition.
Love me like love died with GOOD intention:
That you mustn't have another love after me.
Love me like the blind mute: *Can't hear! See?*

Winding Rode (Botanic African Dove)

I took that wine-N road,
And it led to love's undertakings.
Given all the *Jive Curves,*
I am not shitting - *while shaking.*
I love what I love and
What I love I won't un-love...
We are not just another seedless,
Water Melanin,
We are used to be perceived as ONE -
Botanic African Dove*!*

From Broke to Rich in Just One Weeping Smile

Rain makes me rich.
Water washes *quick*.
Tears thick as blood,
Rower for life flood.

Can't Even Flee a Flea

I Wish Love would chase after me,
Then I'd know *my dogs* are FREE!
I Wish Hate did hang from aTREE!
Fleas feed off the blood of eternity!

I Need That Sane Love to Be Insanely Sane

I need, want AND got to have THAT *someone* –
To whom I might propose to on the telephone,
And then go and buy their only diamond ring.
Someone who takes love on a whirlwind TOUR;
Someone who buys for me my OWN *loves* LOT,
But got the courage to speak up for US and pray:
"Thank You LIFE for giving ALL WE BOTH GOT!"

Feed Me

I hunger for love the ways you lie in your double-crossed FACE,,..
It's like you are waving your flag to start the late *Chariot's* race,,..
And none other can see into those eyes that aren't cocked back,
Or, you're not The Truth that comes all dressed up in *LIGHT black*.

Freed to Go Alone

So glad you are back at home with me,
Know! I do not move when *We're gone*.
I am the one who so loved Your Words:
Freed you from underneath *OUR* stone.

WHERE HAVE *MY* HAND(S) BEEN?!

"COME INSIDE, MY DEAR FRIEND"
('AFTER BEING COLD AND LOST ALONG THE WAY....')
WHERE HAVE YOUR HANDS BEEN?

"HAVE THEY BEEN UNDER ANOTHER'S CUP-LESS BLOUSE?
DIDYOUINVITETHEMINTOTHEDEADWORLDJAIL-HOUSE?

"COME DEEP(ER) INSIDE LOVE NEVER PRETEND WITH A FRIEND...
HAVE YOU BEEN IN TOUCH WITH YOUR WORLD 'a' FULL(Y) FREE?
WHEN DO MY INHERITOR SEND DOWN LIFE SUFFER(ER) FOR ME?
(BUT, YOU DON'T COME NEAR(ER) TO ME FOR ANOTHER ONE OF
MY *POSTPAID*, DUTCH-TREAT-LIKE TOUCH....*ON THE LOW-DOWN)!*

"COME INSIDE, DUSTY 'OLE GRIN WITH THE GLASS(Y) GLASS,
CHINNING-CHIN? (ALL LOCK(ED)-UP INSIDE OF (Y) OUR EMOTION((K)
no(W)-less): ONCE AGAIN...LET'S BEGIN with YOUR god-bless(ed)
SIN: WHERE HAVE YOUR *"GD" ("GOT DIRTY")* HANDS BEEN?

"HAVE THEY BEEN BREW(N) UP ON THE
CORNER WITH YO' KIN(D)?
'CAUSE THE CHILDREN HAVE MILKED THIS PERFECTLY
SOUR(ED) LIFE AND, NOW, HAVE CHURNED THE
DEADS WELL WATERS INTO "GOOD GIN"!!!

Echo:("WHERE HAVE 'OUR' HANDS BEEN"?!
("WE WANNA(S)/GONNA(S) MUST NOT LET US
LAY (1s) HAND(S) ON E(WE)...AGAIN"))

BLACK MALE(R)

Black MALE(R),
White BALE(R),
Dead JAIL(ER)!

MY "X" Married YOUR "Ex" (or "Vice Versa")

                              And...NOW...
BOTH of THEM "is" BECOMETH "one" EXcommunicated....

Passive Voice

I just want this empty feeling to go astray.
I just want this feeling empty to stay away.

"Making This Feeling Die Fresh, Again, Today"

Admittable Then Unforgettable

I know I am not only illegally Blind,
But that don't look like my writings
On the wall.
So, let me help you up,
Nexus time when I fall.
(While some is looking up the 'word,"
Guess what that "Deaf" heard?)
(In the old Country WE couldn't say,
"Deaf " if it didn't rhyme with *"Thief."*)

Kissing Up To The SUN

SUN,
Come and *git yo' lit' bit' blinding tale* back-N*hear*,
And bring all *dim* shade bourne *sunRays* without hue.
Goddamn! The ways *US* dog-gone and fully "*blown up*,"
Smelling real good(s), and still *well-drunk*, under-the-table.
Must be something 'bout (t)hose watered down in the first of
These last *lasting forever* everlasting last *THEYS*!?
Already *new* that one of these *necktimes (next?)*,
And, this wasn't going to be never another *they-too-soon*,
But not so much as it is still too further away after *gooning too far*,
Still sweating that the *SUN* won't stop me from *throw-end*
In-word (only) *back in 2-d-Cell Jail knot again*.
'Course, WE's still *N-deeded-olded* ("*US's owed* ")
Just as certain as do YOUR *cerebellum- less-frontal-brain looks backwards*....
"Oh, What Amply Hot Times We Have Waiting (room) in The *Cold Sore Sun*!"
(Death cannot defend the *suns' medicating, chilling truths*....)
How's *BIG HEAT STROKING*? Still smiling ("beaming") on
On these lifeless little *dark-pesky-greys*?
And what's up with the *precipitation* for those other,
Too sorrowfully slow *burning-out, unrested* heaters?
One *MELTING* truth *about sunsetting in the FALL*:
"HELL could never deny giving the *WORD* the warmest *global warning*:
Just Cause lovers of the rehidden Life love like
The *Long-Gone-Runner* WILL be the first ONE to win unforgivable grace -
Some wanna be dead Knee-Grow-Crawling with a Cross *(beau)*,
Double-Crossing death at the *finish-lying*,
Re-buckling from a day of being chased by *Blue Faded Fools*....
Shoo!!!...."

                ("Verily"! "Verily"! "Verily"!)

SUN, I Do Dread Having to Re-Borrow My *Diss*Own Flowers Re-Back From Heaven Again, *Child*

You might make me jump,
But I bet you that I *will never*
(make that "won't ever")
Jump as high as you'll jump,
When dangling in front of me,
Like a Heaven-*Dread*!
When I make me the "up-Jumper,"
You will be the *Flours-Self-Rising in*
Hell House, Light-Bread!?!?!?

ReLoading for My Next to the Last Laugh *(Just Case for a Calling)*

If all that you are going to do is weep, *baby*,
Just Cry Laughing.
I'm not dying to have the Laughters Last Laugh.
That would be like saving your own dead SOUL.
Get that *good dinner* and Coupon-quarter-back
(40 days, 40 acres, 40 ounces),
Then when you should be re-huddled on that UP,
Passing Sack.

The Things Seen

I saw an ambulance following a hearse.
It should have been the chase, not *grin*!
That the dead cannot drive in a r*everse*.

I saw a *hearse* waiting for its *ambulances*,
Except the wait was for the ride in HEARSE....
Life has foretold that it takes *Last Chances*.

More Than Less Given

I gave more than was given to patroit *Me*.
But You did not yourself, come back - see!?

Character Witness

Life need no complicit witness
For the Soon to be Departing!
Life consummate with Deaths;
They testify against each other
      BY OUTSMARTING....

Enough to Have Gone Around

My Mama could take one slice of light bread,
Sufficiently teasing the *tasties* of her children,
CHILD!!!!!!
With HER African-Gold-Chain, eroping NILE,
She can rebirth more gods and goddesses,
Than that delvish rat - *"COON"* could never defile.
("Running around on *moi* (do "choose me, *pretty papa*").
Even the wicked must have FUN!
But why must it always be lit' bit' sunnies
On blast with that *good-ducking-looking SUN?*
(And I say WE are not finished yet....)
There is not enough *sun-tan-ocean,*
Unless you are rowing with the motion....
Yo' mammy told lies for SUM-CUM and
Cold-Weather-Women, like they couldn't lose
Their "w" and become a mere "omen" (B-Knot-*N Days Name*).
If I thought I could forever (eternally, and foreverlast-inLife2) WIN,
Still wouldn't play to *pay* yo' GAME.
And to all the sun lovers, Forgive me (ass-well),
Cause I pray not SAY:
This is how eye gets through 2-1 of Life's
Fucked-Up-Theys!!!

The Every-Day Life

The every-day life is a walking blues,
Stranger to the integrity of *miss-hues*.
The Every-Day-Life fears nothing nor
Anybody, but knows days are AFAR.

That "Oscar" Buzz

Each time I see You,
I hear the Oscar buzz.
You acting like love isn't
What life lived it to be:
Prison...

That "Oscar" Buzz!!!

Each time we act like
We are not acting,
The Performance of love.
Oscaring free like a *bird*,
Does....

The Good Night Folk (Whether Prosecution or Persecution, *WE* Did Not Get No Justice, COOL!)

I would not prosecute My FAMILY of friends.
Nor would I persecute the ones that pretend.
I love with a heart full of truly purity in its love,
(And this is not another one of *SUN-heat-joke*)
The last to go will be the *good, gone, dark folk*.

No Trouble Double-Taking Application (Double Time For Snoring)

Said, EWE, You don't want *no more* trouble.
Then, We get paid for snoring times, double.

There is No Limit to Perfectioning a Time Limitation

There is a time Limited to Perfection.
Perfection's the *Sin of MissDirection*.

Too, Too, Too

I was reading my *thinking* thoughts:
Wearing little blinders, *gone* - *WALK!*
("Because some can only *slang* dirt")
See what waiting while you work can do?!
(I can't see digging US down to the black and *BLUE*,
But WE, too, got, some shoveling up, again....
To Do2....

Cornered, Amen! Cornered, Amen! Cornered Amen! (Only Partial)

Let's *hallelujah* this deaf-N Chorus,
And don't just sit in Amen's Corner.
Whether staying in or dropping out,
Cannot be the same as *this* Goner.

Do You Need Me? *(Why Grey isn't Gray?)*

One Day!?
I will be too gone!
Did you another sentiment,
Other than "So Long?"
Do you truly need me,
To continue "holding it down?"
What if I am already underground?
One Way?!
Then, redirect My heart.
Until the Sun throws *shade*
On another day.
Do you need me?
Why question my stay!?
This is less of a question,
No more than *"Grey isn't Gray"*?!

THE KNIGHT IS HEAVIER ON HORSES

May I invite you to spend a night
Within my daydream?
You can See the stare of the DAY;
Mine are night mean!

Basking off Into That SUN

SUN,
I CANNOT dehydrate a water-drop,
Not with My HOT-SUN-OF-A-GUN.
The SUN can dehydrate SUMMER,
But, SUN LOVES its WINTER FUN.

My Back Time

You got me disbelieving that I'm
Just time up from the vying.
I cannot get back my *back* time,
Swearing while *Back's* cryin'.

The SUN Cannot Hold Its *Liquored*

Living shouldn't be a *Liquored Death*.
Hate being a little tipsy, no disrespect.
One can find the SUN under the table,
Looking like *a recovered from disabled*.
Imagine helping the SUN to get on up?
I'd rather be emancipated where I *SEE*
Whose DNA is burning in DOA icy CUP....

I've Traveled

I've travailed through the depths of hell,
Colder than the heat that is *brain-swell!*

Hot Damned

Do not blame the rash of outbreaks on the SUN.
This SUN takes scorching orders from *LIL' GUN*.
GUN says SHOOT! And SUN answer: *HOT? Hi!*
If this *SUN* were your *grave-filling Urn*, you'd die.

Much Too Much

Much too much is less than never Enough.
Much too much is shorter than life's *HUSH*.

When Do I Become The Beloved?

I speak with enunciations drowned in the well.
I'm not the bespoken of nor the love foretelled.
Love me like a lover who loves without love-jail.
When do I become a beloved, needing no bail?

Though Active

When life stop giving out A Reward,
You will win.
Know Your performance's unnatural,
Pretending.
Tell US that you do not miss practice,
Death Acts!
Like life's not complicit, *though active*.

Those Many Features ("MFs") in You, Bro? (or 2 little MFNs W/O "Melanin")

This peace should be renamed,
Uncensor *My Fictions (still "MFs")*!!!
Come, "spend the night in my dream."
In my dream, the SUN does not burn
They brother....

Misappropriation of Sin

I don't accept, as fact, that my days are done....
I don't accept, as *Act*, misappropriation of sin,
SUN.

Never Defined

I stepped into a world,
Unlike any this world had before.
Never quite known.
In this world,
I am a baby, but
Must act grown,
Which is never defined.
In this world,
I am fully grown,
But hanging
By the embibli cord's pre-conception.
And still,
Won't face the *SET-UP-SUN*,
Like I'm not an insightful, *BLIND*.

A Master's Piece

Give me All,
Because EVERYTHING is
Pre-served to THEE!
Death shall split the "SEE"
AGAIN,
And then love will conquer
ETERNITY.
YOU will inherit it ALL,
Even temperaturizing the WEATHER....
Only a hot-tempered-fool
Gets to die, so
UNJEALOUS!!!

The SUN Made Me Mad

Did Hell break out, again?
You ain't gonna never get
Mr. Charlie locked back in.

Does the *SUN* wear *Dark*?
Mr. Charlie will always TRY
To suffocate by *death mark*.

If First Paul Had Truly Seen The SUN **(or,** "The Fire is Coming!" "The Fire is Coming!" "The Fire is Coming!"

What becometh of the Fire, Paul?
"After burning Gentile's 40th Acre,
Taught them the Knee-Burn-Crawl"!

Misty Hope

Give me liberation from this death.
Give my *Misty Hope* his last breath.

Dark Day Light

Sun, if you want me,
Come and go re-shine on *Your back aching blacks*.
("I know not that both hands Love hasn't shone....")
But my heart does confess during its walk alone...:
That Darkness is in its truest blindness, given my bones,
While the Light still wishes for glow, though overloaded
And *blown*....

A-Man-C-Patients (Emancipation)

You Were a Wailer of a Weeping Star (and "If I Didn't Love You, I'd still believe that *Love* is crazy enough to let you be thinking that you could be going down to finish being the burning feed for *My Load,* THE Whaler, and the bit' lit' SUNNY, Sun, suns")

You were forever the eternalized boy-child-*star,*
Long before I began doing your lit' bit' singing.
Gone like a comet(h) from *Hell's-Holey-Pa Pa,*
Wishing upon night *Peeps who-is-they* dreaming.

The K(night) Wrapper Done Thinking About Dropping Out *of They* School (again?)

Education is the CALL for celebration.
Without education one gets *Re-TURN*.
But with the celebration for the elation,
The SUN can only show *HELL BURN*....

That's No Reason to Leave Somebody Behind

That's no reason to be leaving no *body*,
Just because you are running lit' Tardy.

Blown Horn

Hell serves barb-be-cue chicken
With thorns.
Let the cock suckers sound alarm:
Blow Horns!!!

Children

I fell but I'm alright,
Children of the Child!?
So goddamn pissy drunk,
Goal? "Road to Denial"!
Sipped my will for *over poor-ed—CUP ("Old-englih, britNvoice",)*
Children of THE NILE!
Like I beg children not to re-dirt their Child:
Tears pour down my CUP!
As BAD as GOOd US is (KNOT),
What's wrong with KneedN?
A lit' bit' sub-assistance
Just gettin' The Lover of *One* Life
On the *Catch-UP (Hot Dog! Blood and Water Mix)*....

Restoration

Penetrate the imagination,
Pray to find your *adorable*.
Let your fear heed its nest,
The plate's anorexic-proof....

Too Deep a Digging for the *Pie-Rotter's* Free Silver (Pyrite's Gold)

Too Deep for me?
Not the hole,
But the hold
On one's SOUL.
Too Deep for me!
Not just the
Slippery-Wine-N-Road,
But, Also,
The load, leading to
Pyrite's Gold.

Probationary Massa Degrees of the Dying *Kissers Uppers*

Don't you fire off on that new *Boss*!!!
US Patients got to be keeping up with this here next *JOB*.
Just because somebody's anorexic glutton,
Ated away at all of the *innocent* doves' bruised hearts.
Don't be going up *where* making them same new *landlords*
Good-Old-Boy, New Dead Slobs....

Slipping on The Guarded Blade

Why doesn't the *SUN day* provide shade?
Why is heat hotter than hell's oven burns?
Why is the sword cleansed from its blade?
Why doesn't the SUN *fall* doing *RE-Runs?*

Dark Beauty

Dark beauty is darker than
Light Beauty,
Which is lighter than *Dark*.

Dark Beauty is lighter than
Light Beauty,
Which is the *Darkest Heart*.

Sky By Night

In Our sky by night,
We see the day travel from
Darkness to its Light.
We know that the siblings of a
Crescent Moon burn.
While ALL rotate mythologically,
Another One will get their *URN*.

That Love Knew

Love Knows this *Wretched*
Paradise was understated,
After exonerating Heaven,
Black Hell's been Berated!!!

A Brand-New Dance for Novelty

You place a second hand over...,
And stop that *stalking* clock (be nice for *a charge!*).
Then, after you light the tick,
You may dance with the *ROCK* (permission granted, if not *stoned*).
                Traitor! (clock)!!!
Does the Traitor commit to a heavenly Treason,
Or does loving Traitor displaces for hell's eternity?
If some are planning to take back their freedom
Right away, come first chance they get tomorrow,
Is it POSSIBLE to have less *LATER-Day-sorrow*?
If all Traitors must commit undying love to Treason,
Whom would Treason dare kiss to die *Traitor True*?
Can old Traitor run and stowaway without Treason,
If dying to be a Traitor, living with death is on YOU!!!

DAY IS ON "D" THEY TIME(R)(S)

YOU DO NOT GIVE US THE TIME,
TO MAKE UP (Y)OUR OWN TIME!
WE DON'T NEED TAKER O' TIME!
DEAD WILL FIND MADE UP TIME!

TWO SPEEDING TICKETS

"ONE TIME I WAS TOO LATE TO GRIEVE"

"ONE TIME WAS TOO EARLY TO LEAVE"

Judas' Cheese

("DEAD RATS CHASE MICE DOWN THE SEW(ER) ON KNEES....")
("WE DIE THE MUTE(D) ON (Y)OUR MOUSE HOUSE CHEESE....")

EYE-C-EWE...zzzzzzz

TALLEY...ho'

Pay They!!!

What Heaven!?

"WHY LIVE TO DO THAT WHICH YOU ARE NOT DYING TO DO?"

ABOUT THE AUTHOR

Andrew Marshall, Jr. was born and raised in Columbus, Georgia, and also attended Claflin Elementary School, a formerly segregated public school that is approximately 145 years old. Claflin Elementary School consisted of grades kindergarten through sixth. Coincidentally, the Author's father, Andrew Marshall, Sr., also attended Claflin as a child growing up in Columbus. Andrew Marshall, Jr., was a student in the last sixth grade class at Claflin, immediately prior to Columbus, Georgia experiencing mandated integration of this Nation's public school systems.

In June 1976, after completing his junior year, the Author graduated from high school. In December of the same year, when he was still 17 years old, Andrew enlisted in the United States Marine Corps (USMC). Prior to leaving for Boot Camp, he made an attempt to count every house and/or lots (where a home had once stood) that he could remember having lived during his upbringing. Subsequently, he counted 13 different home locations. After conferring with an older sister on this number, *that* sister told him that he had missed two other houses. The Author is capable of recalling practically every day of his life.

Andrew Marshall, Jr. had a once in a lifetime experience when he met and conversed with one of history's greatest literary giants of poetry, Miss Gwendolyn Brooks, who was the first African American to win the Pulitzer Prize for her book *Annie Allen* (poetry). Reverently, this chance meeting and brief discussions with Miss Gwendolyn Brooks have been the motivation for some of Andrew Marshall, Jr., more poignant allegorical and metaphorical writings (satirical as well). Additionally, this Author has historically embraced the writings of Langston Hughes, Paul Lawrence Dunbar, along with many of the other notable Harlem Renaissance Writers. With respect to this literary field of endeavors, AndrewMarshall, Jr. has read and/or attempted to analyze the works of many other authors, whether contemporary or historical.

Andrew Marshall, Jr., graduated in 1983 with honors from Bethune-Cookman University (formerly, "Bethune-Cookman College"), an *HBCU* or Historically Black College or University, and has earned a Masters Degree in Human Resources Management and Development. He is a member of Kappa Alpha Psi Fraternity, Incorporated. Additionally, Andrew Marshall, Jr, retired from the United States Federal Civilian Service. The subject book *Lit' Bit'* is a *"SATIRE" (or, satirically **done**)!?!?!?!*

www.ingramcontent.com/pod-product-compliance
Lightning Source LLC
Chambersburg PA
CBHW030549080526
44585CB00012B/310